This Coloring Book Belongs To :

Copyright 2019 Glamorous Ghizlane Maaloum

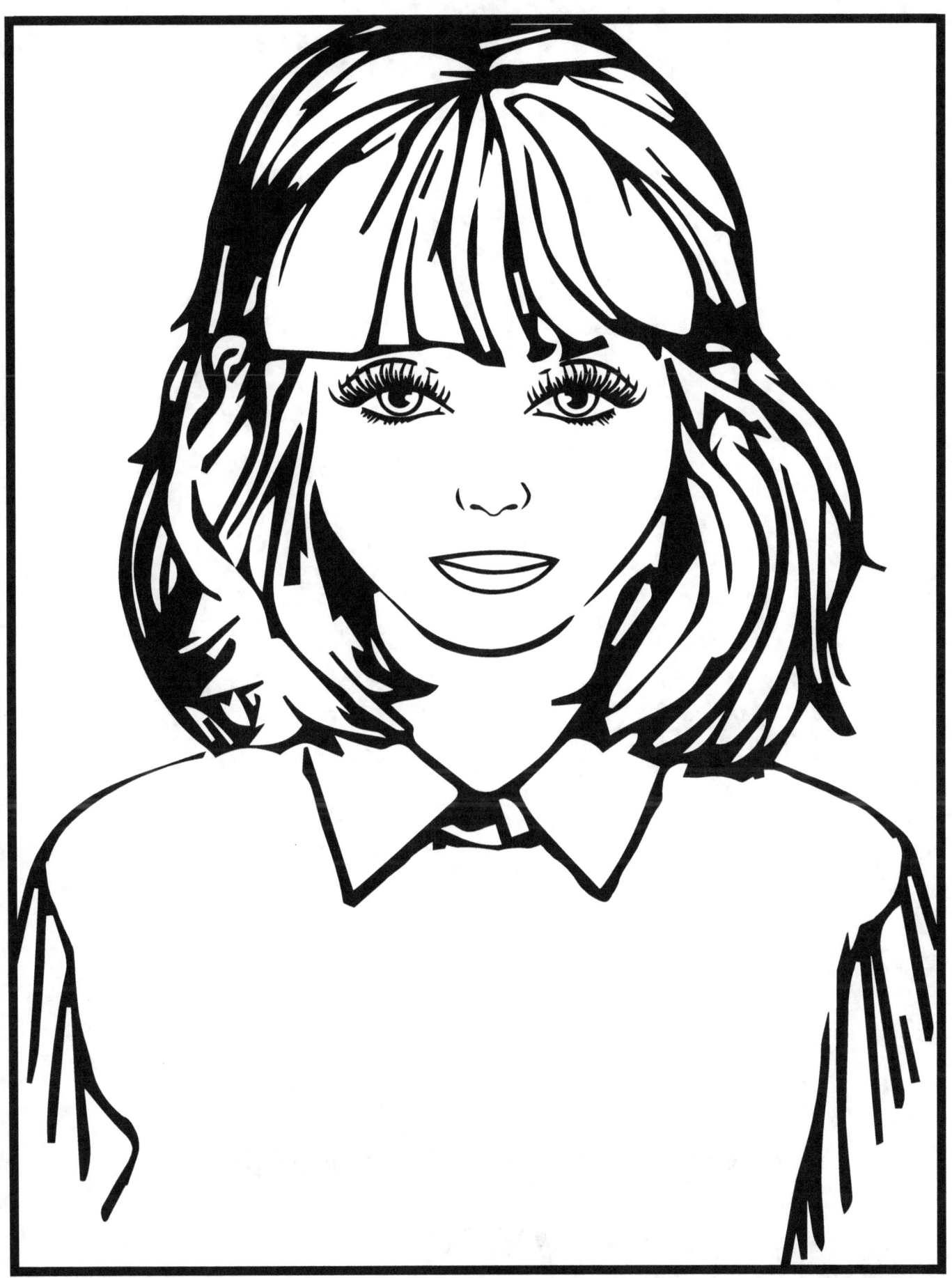

Make up for the evening party

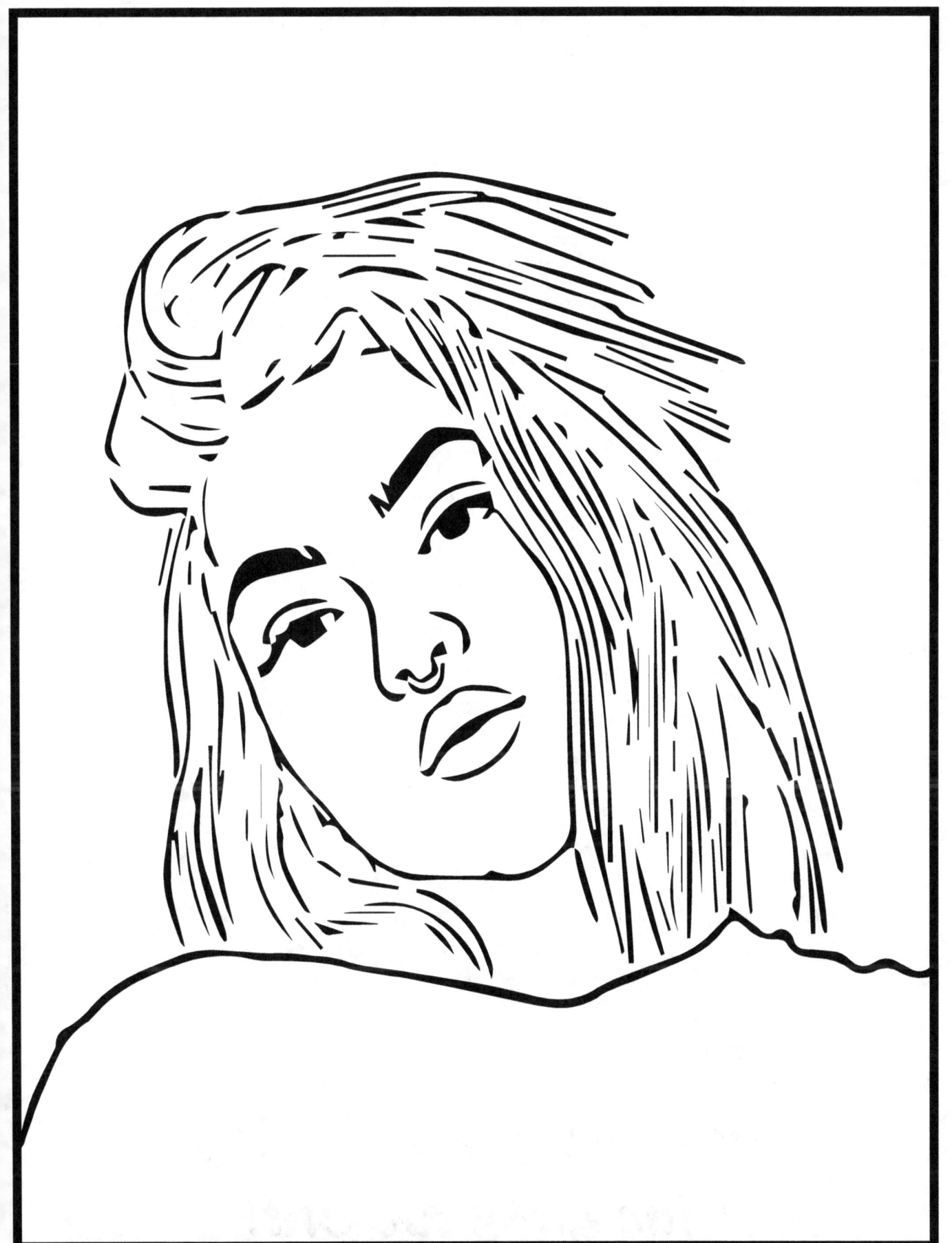

make up for Saturday:
the girls are out!

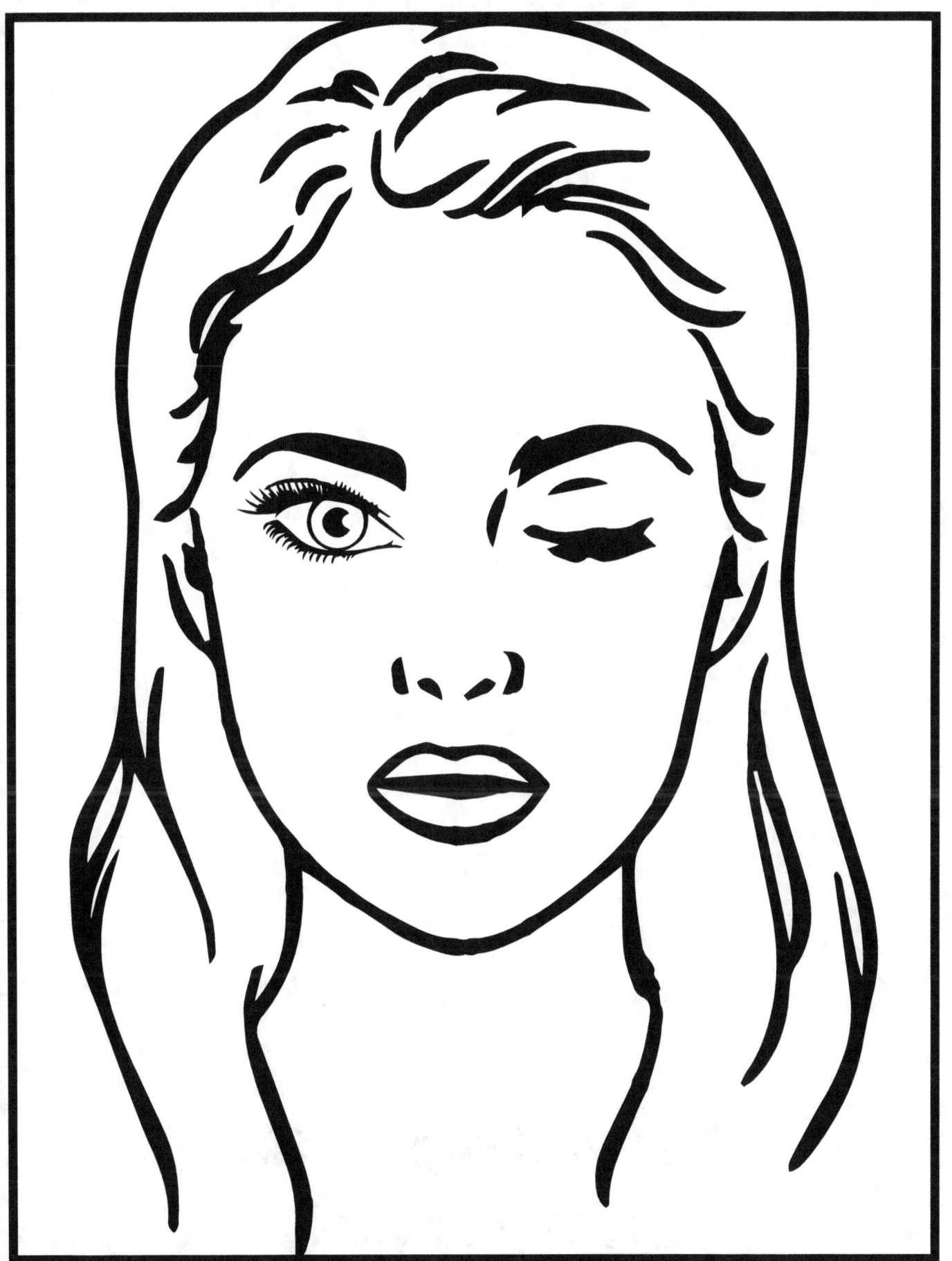

The makeup of the working girl

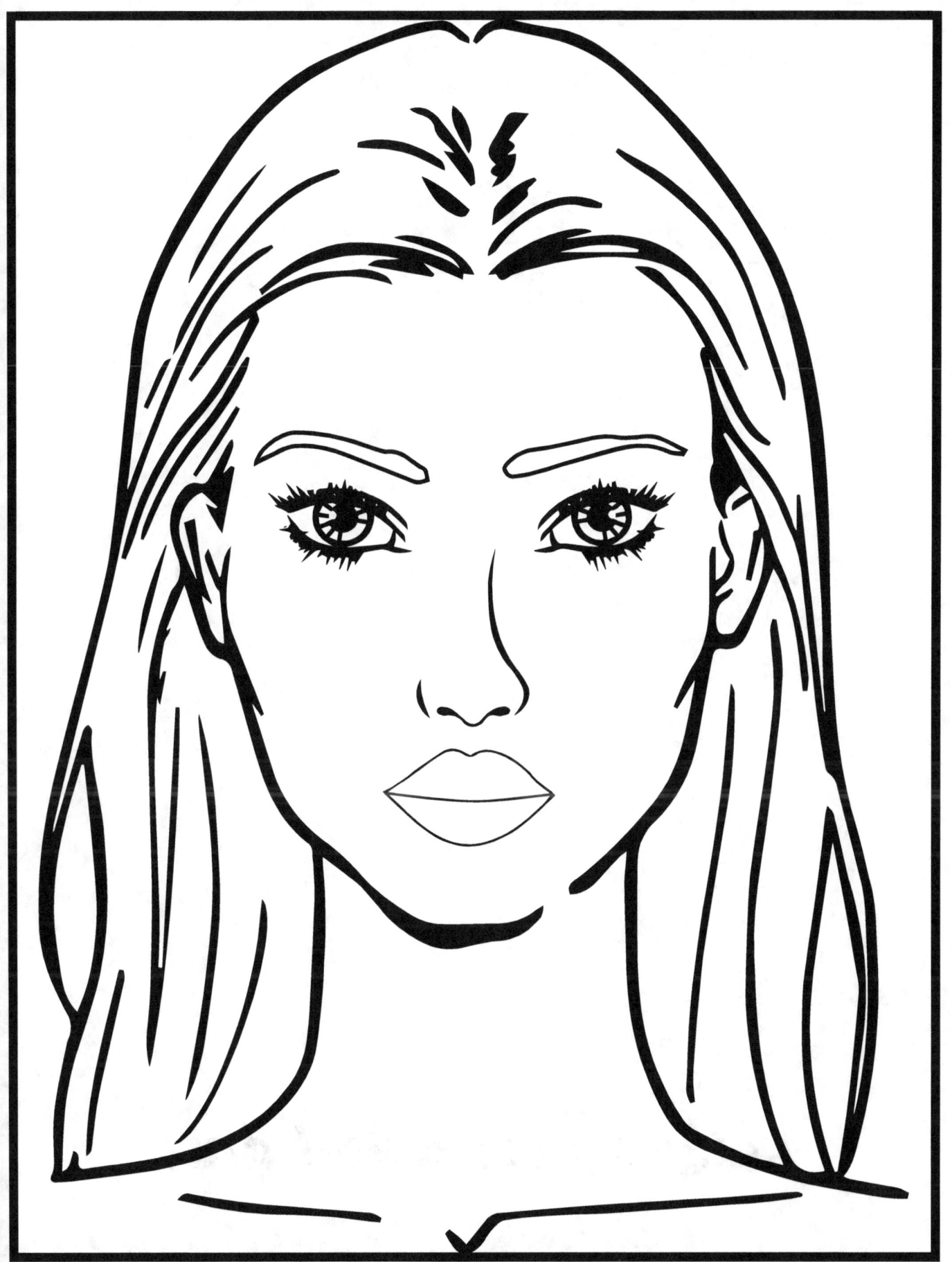

make up for a first date

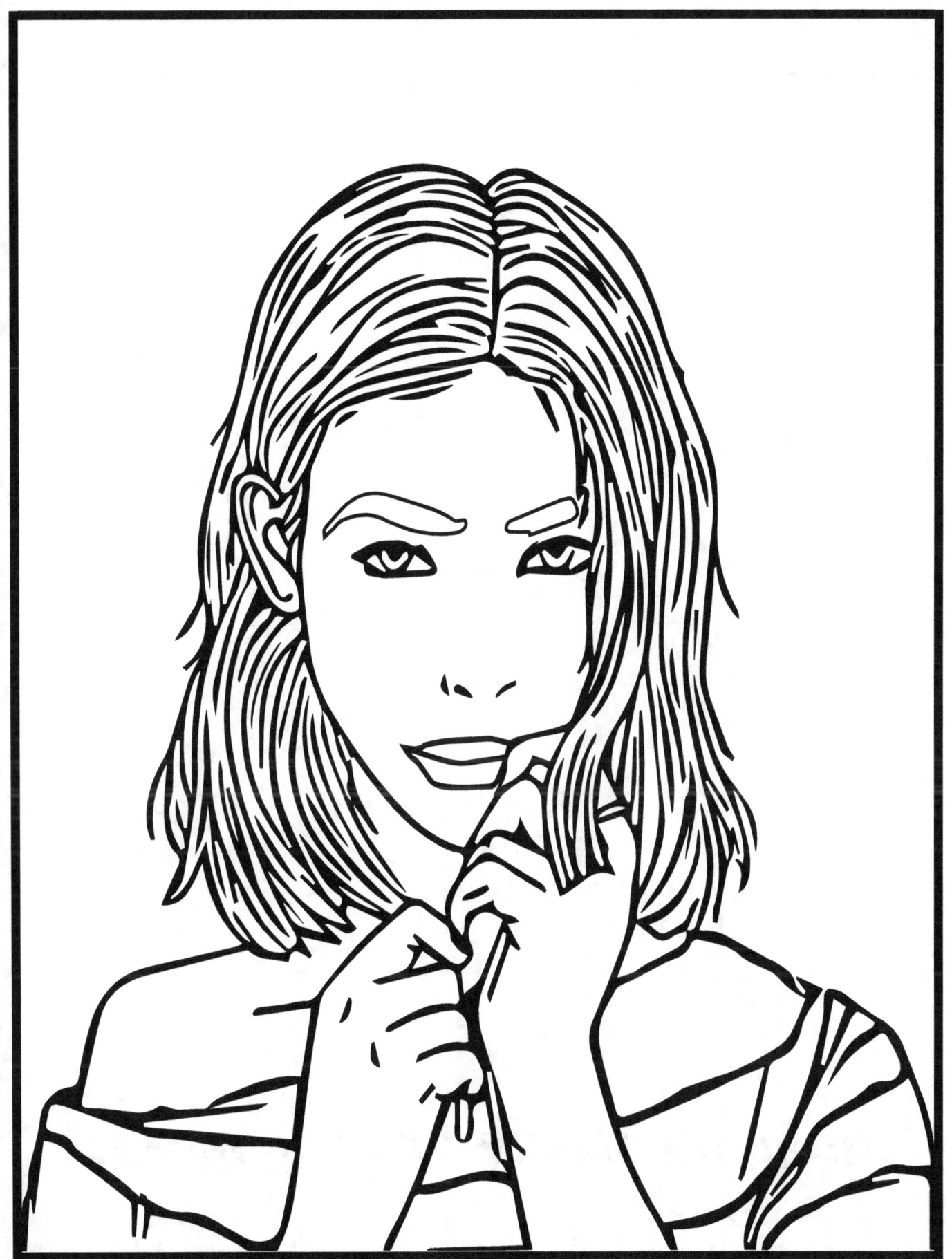

make up Sunday at the market

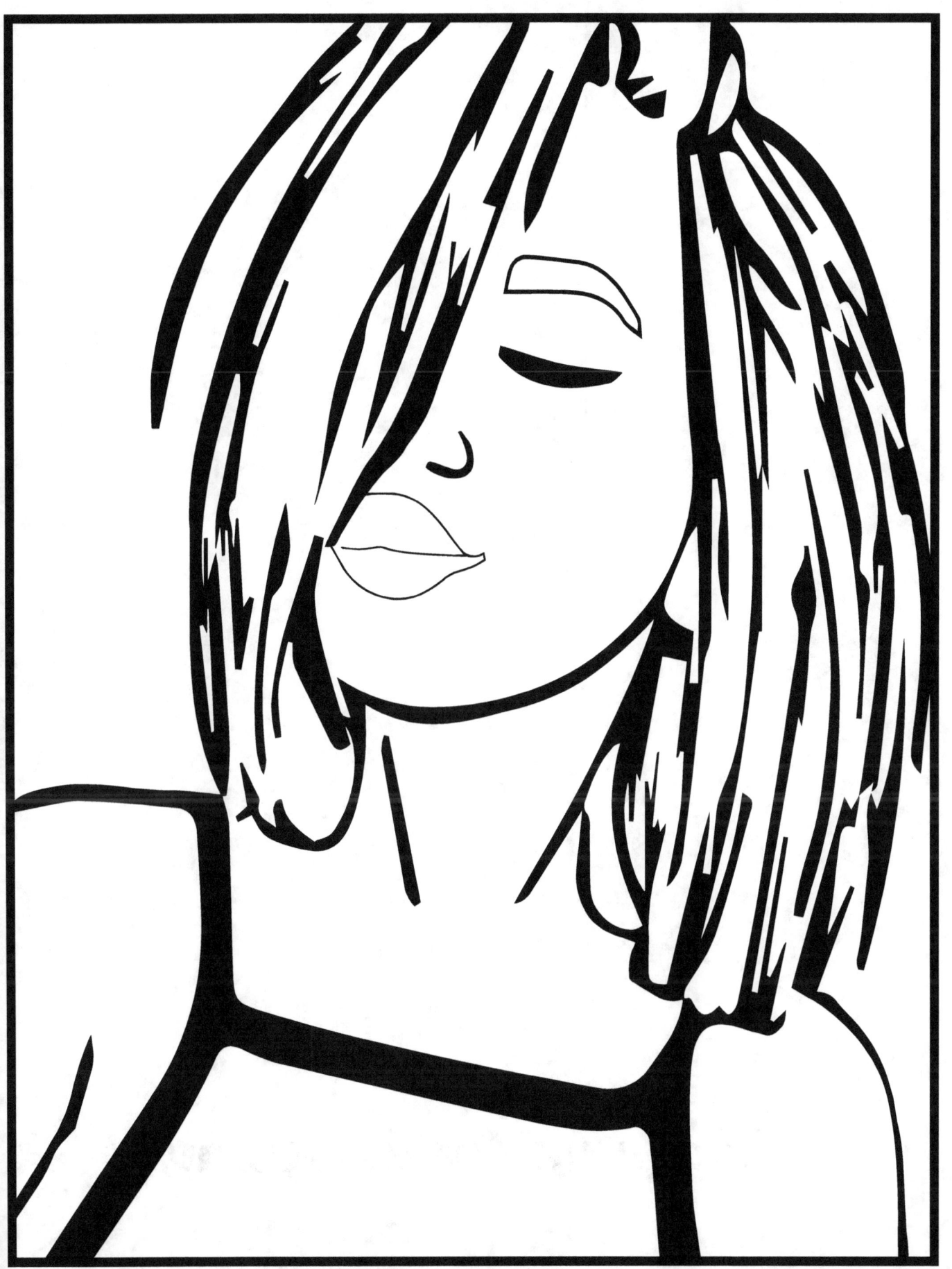

Make up for Everyday

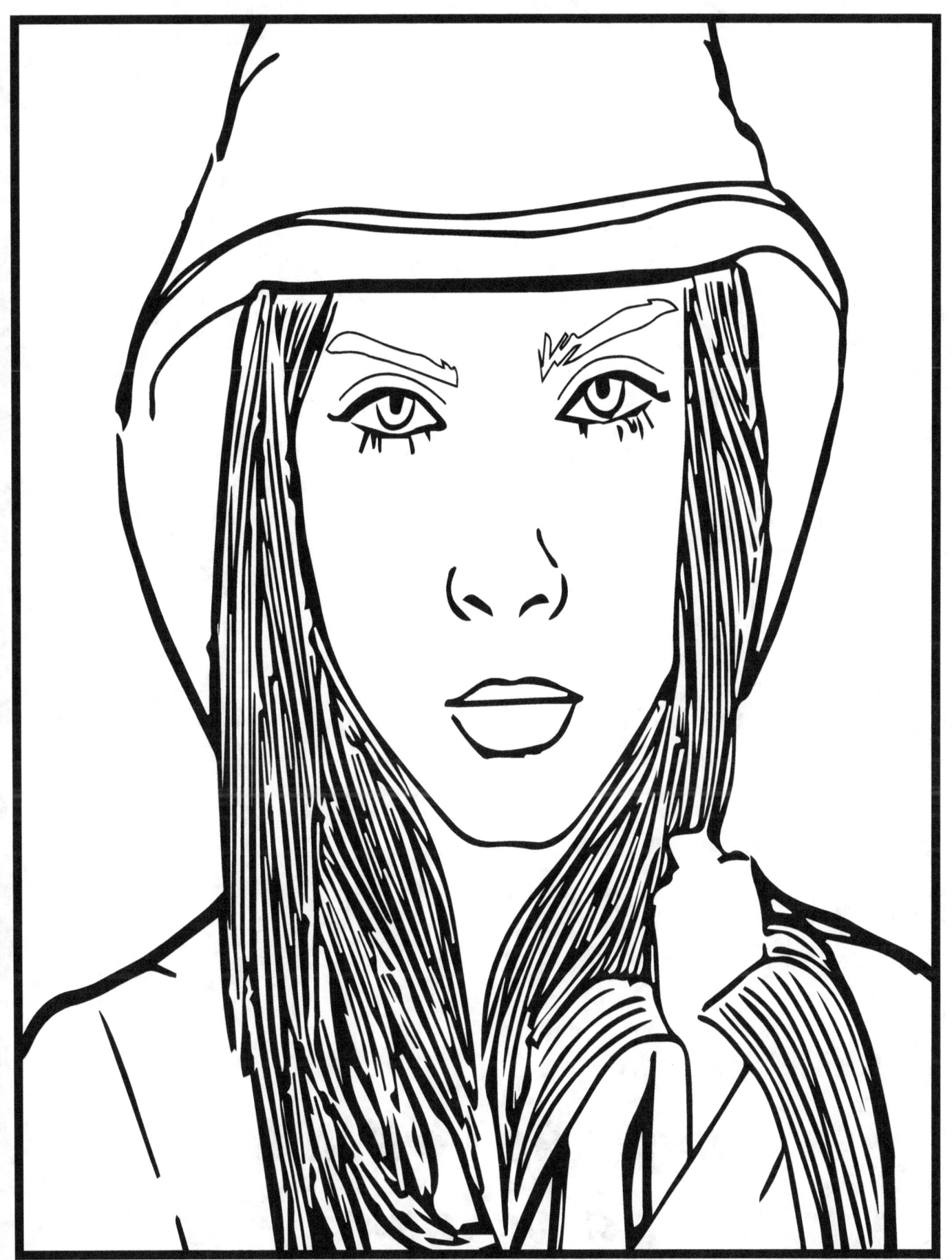

make up invited to a wedding

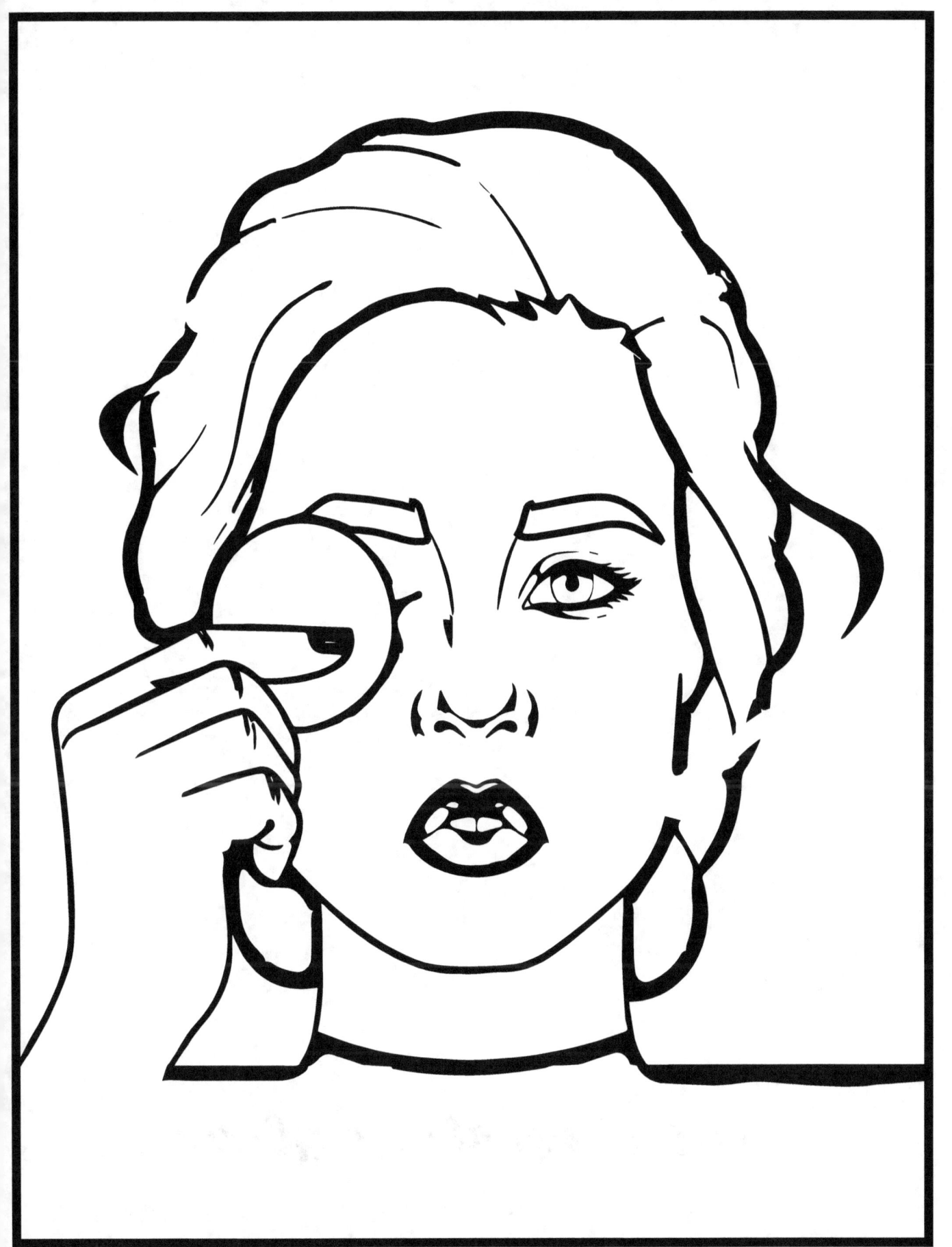

Make up effect glow

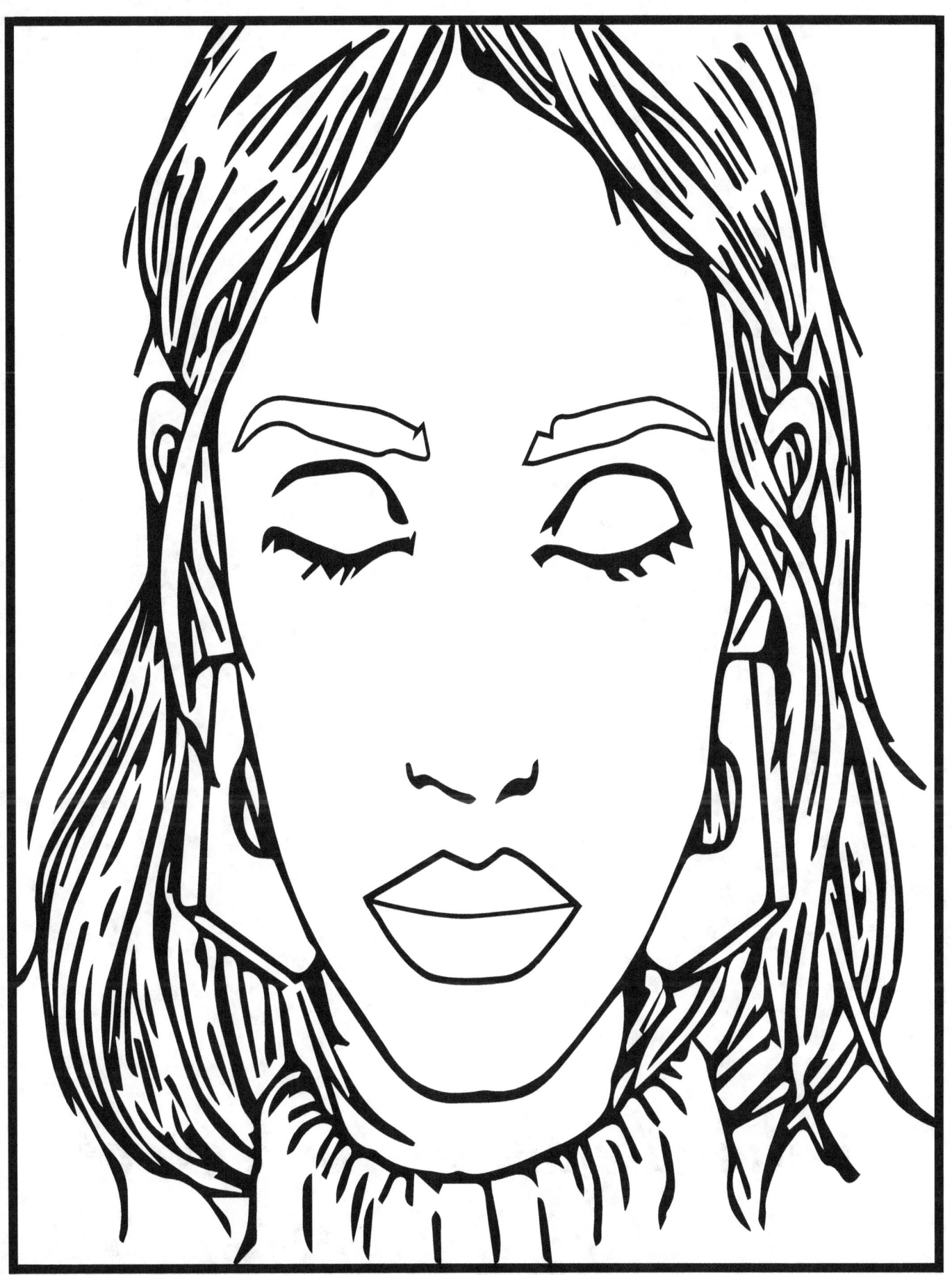

Natural make up for a shoot

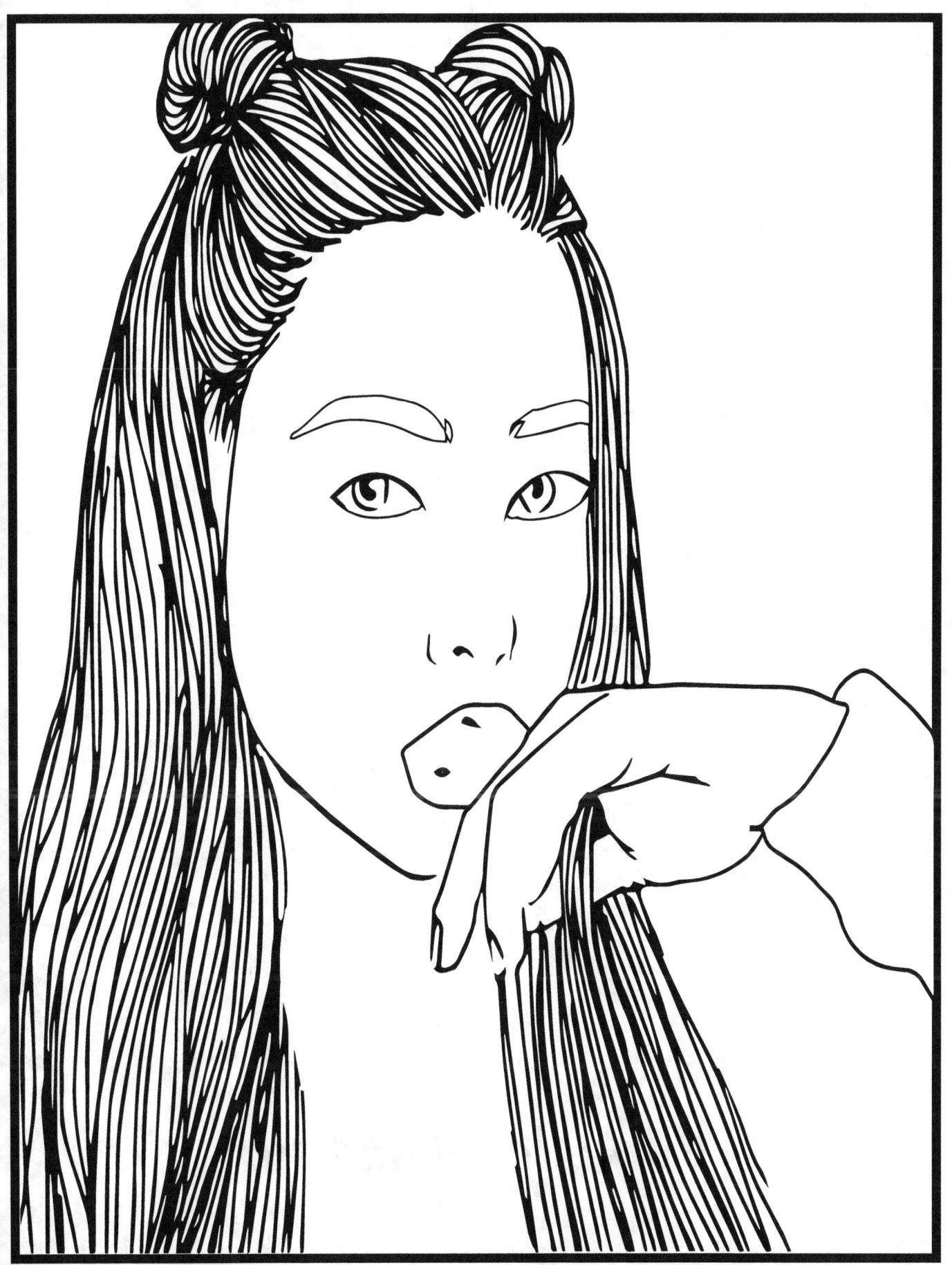

Classic Make up

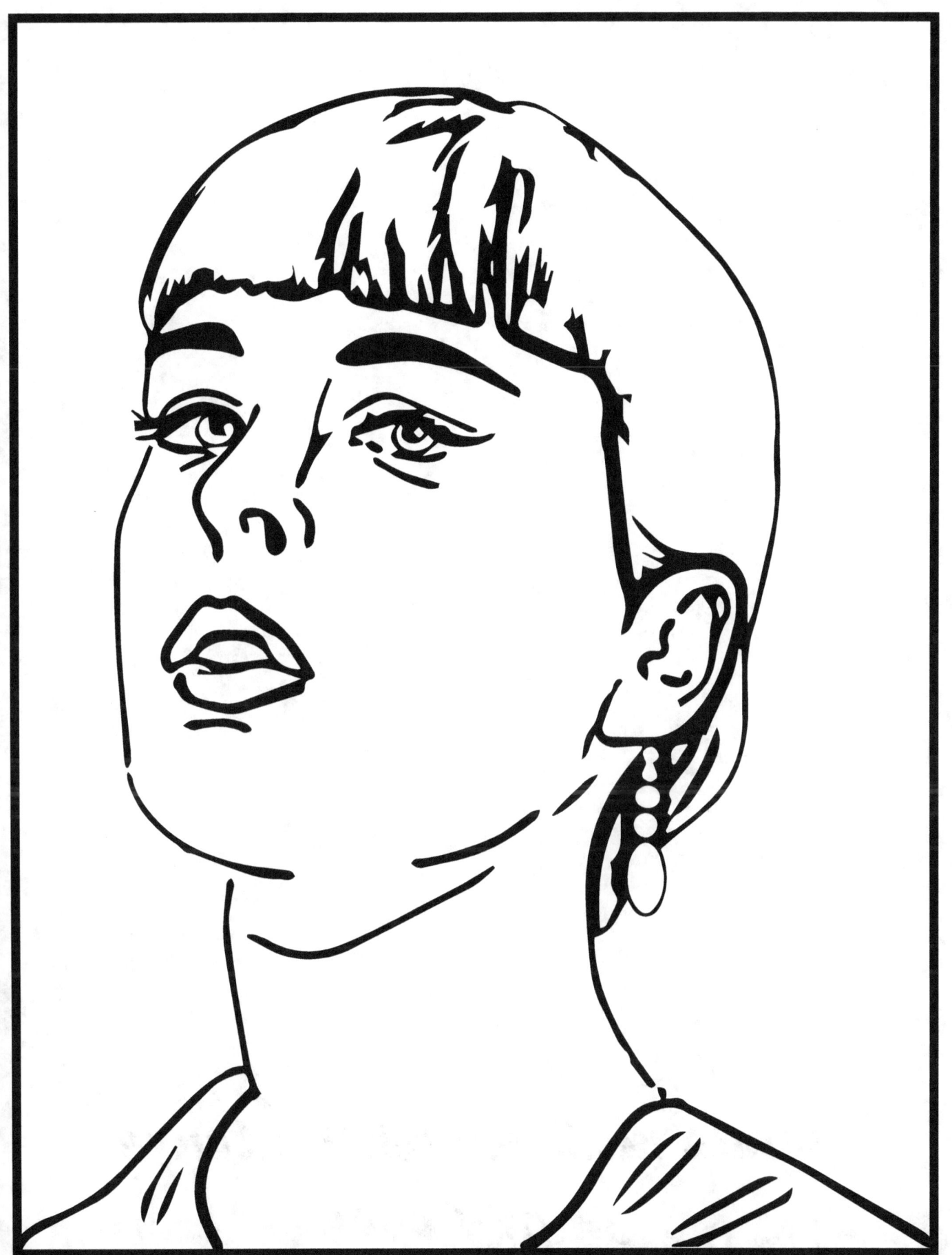

Nude makeup with intense smoky eyes

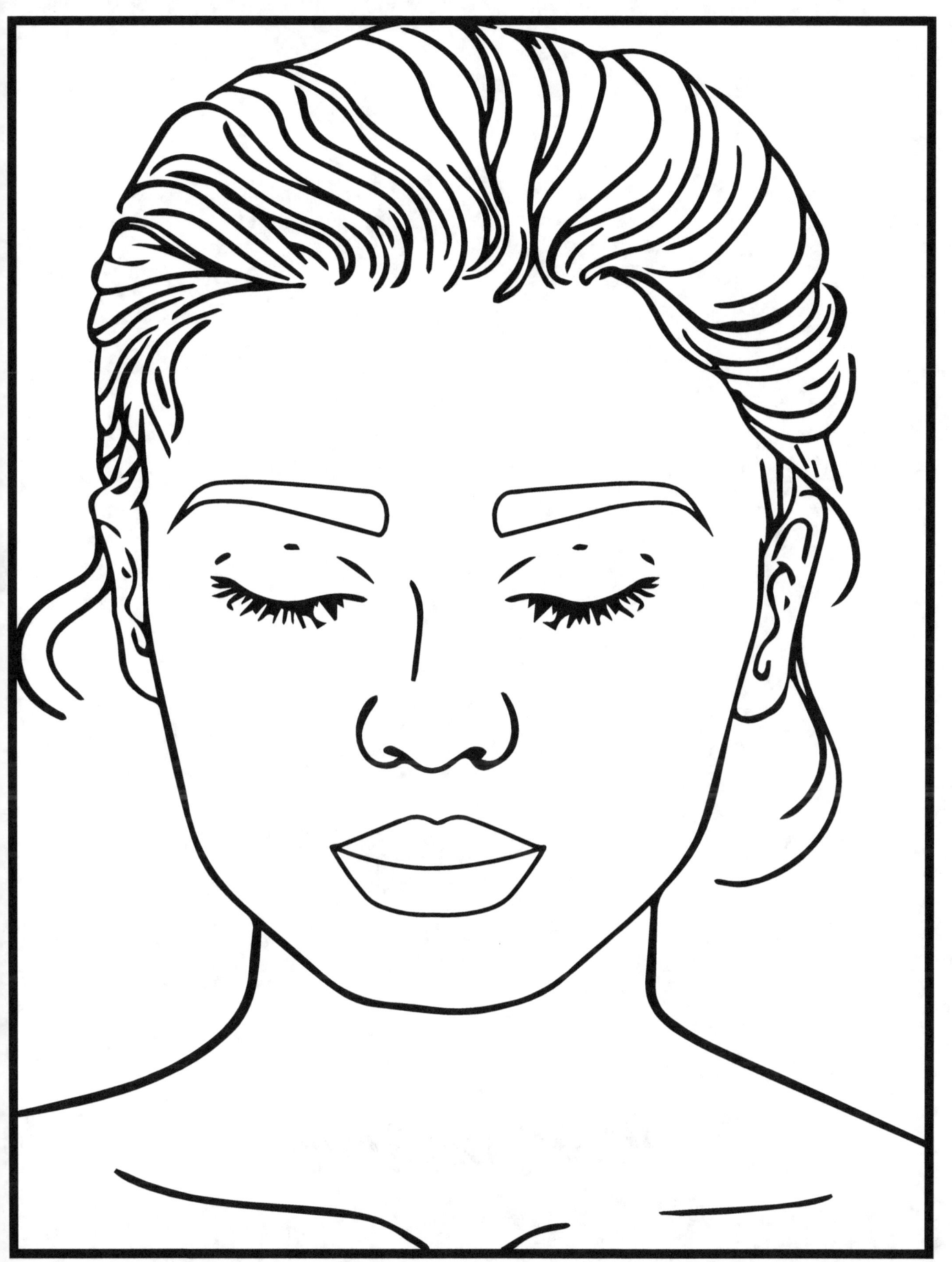

Work makeup

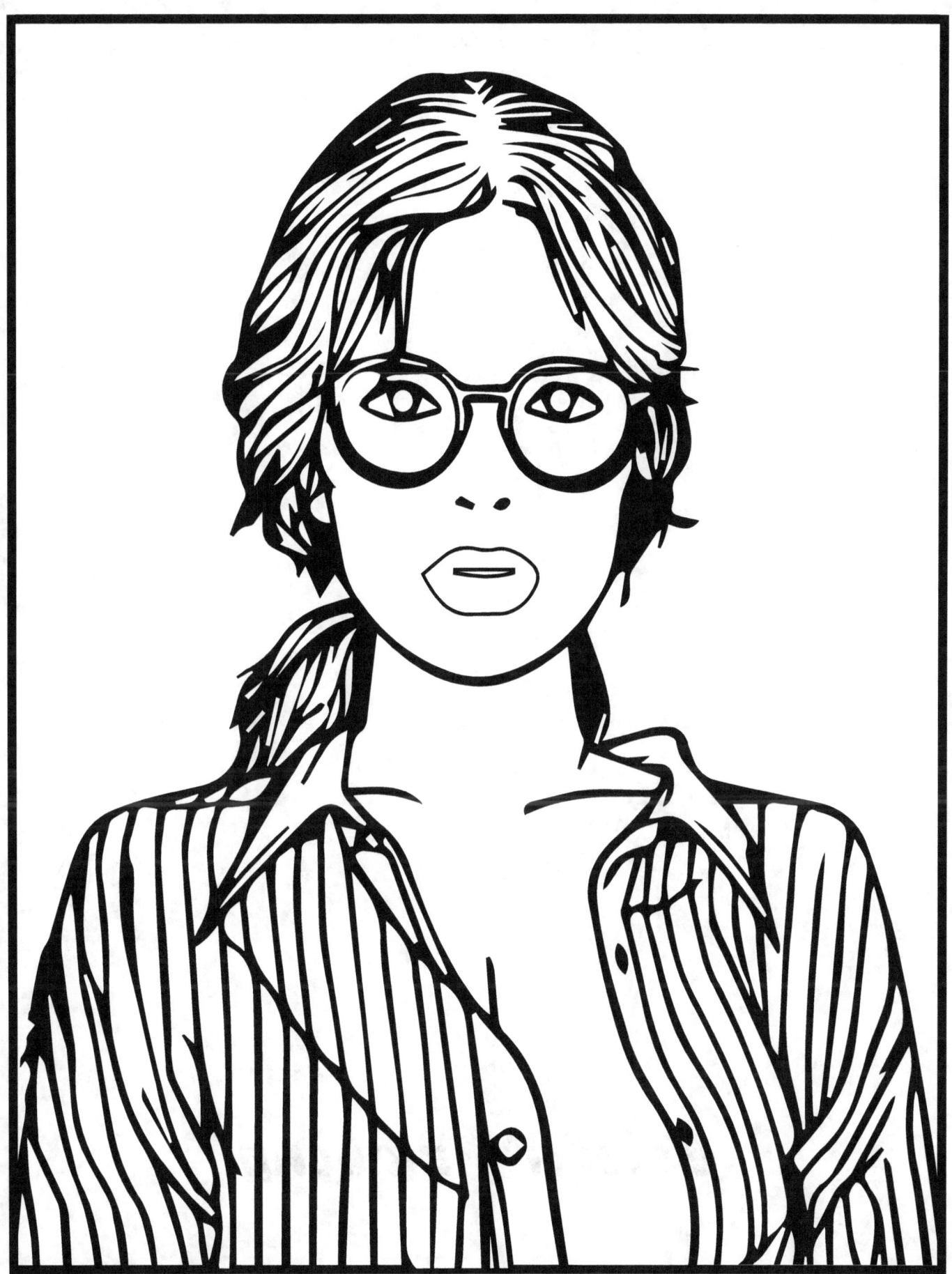

Celebrity makeup

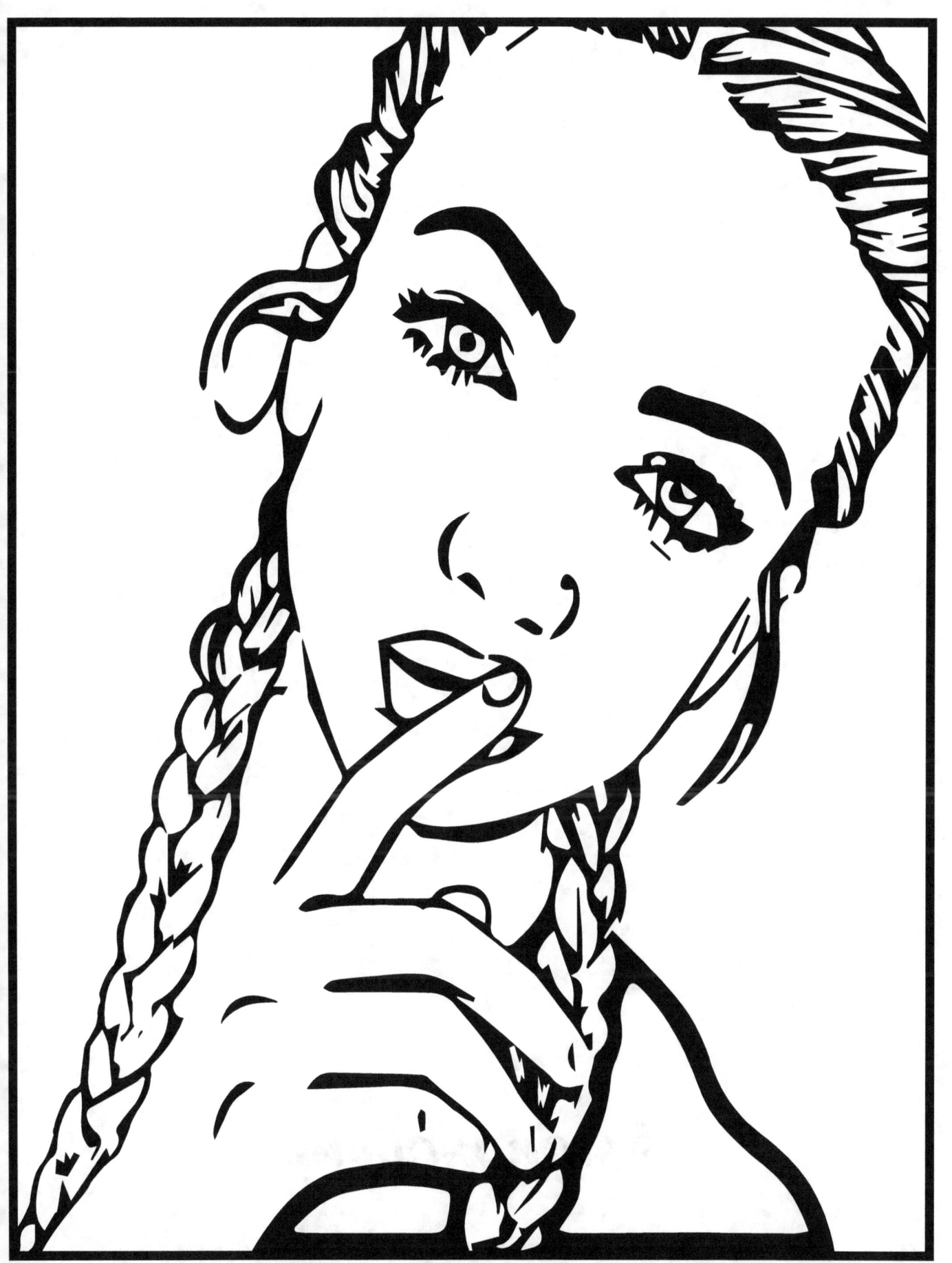

Asian makeup

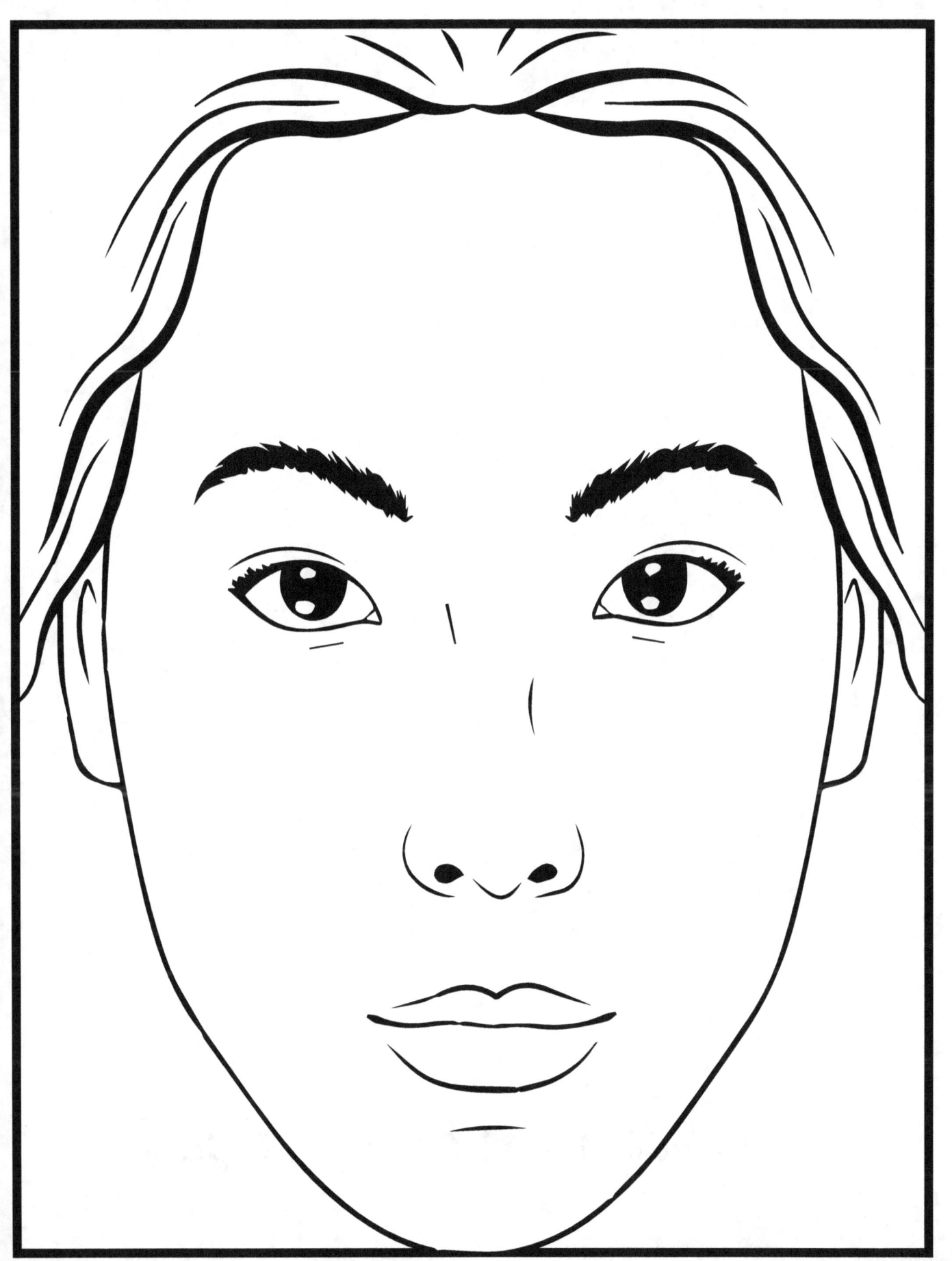

Makeup for teenage girl

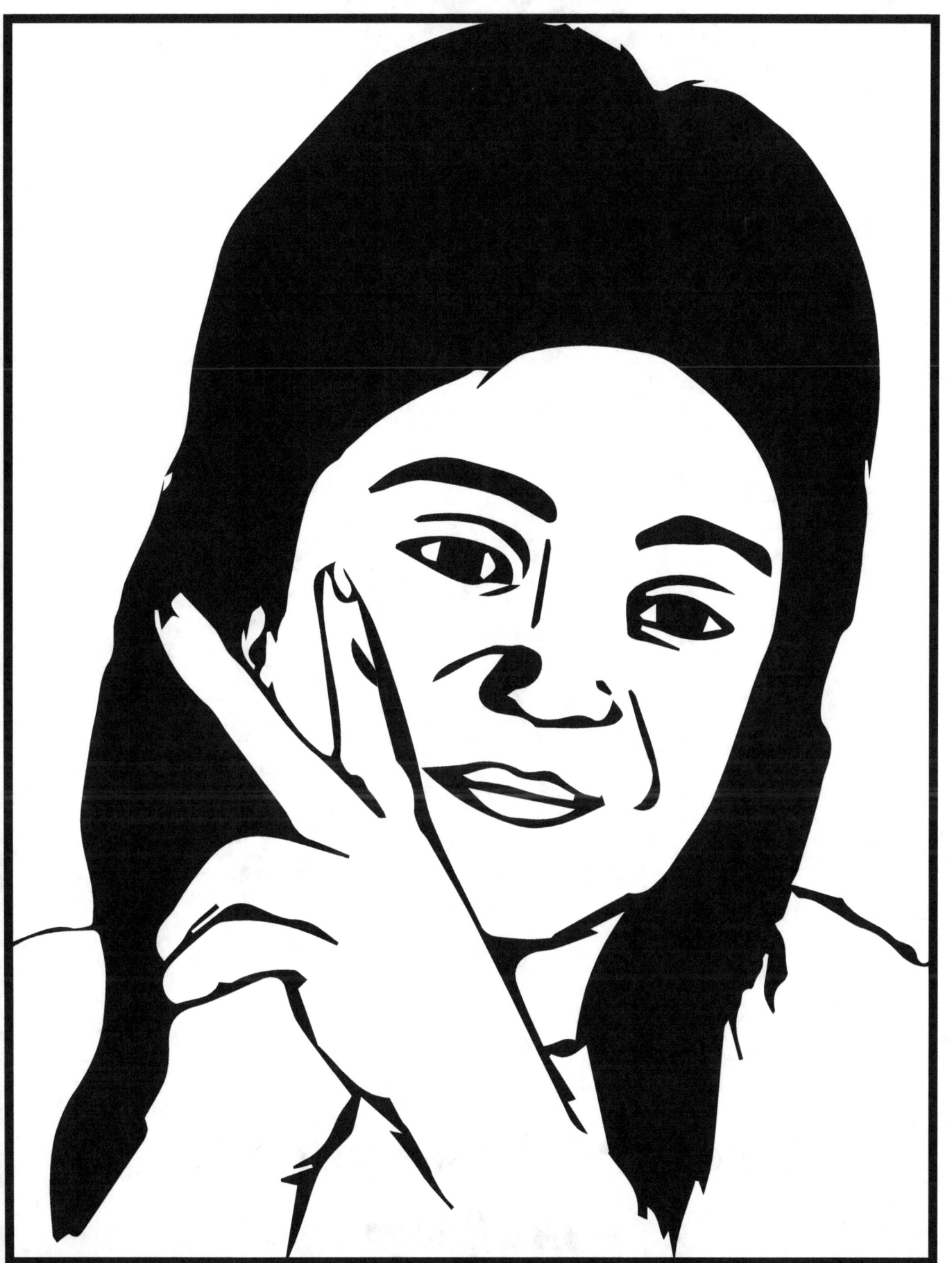

Very soft and simple makeup

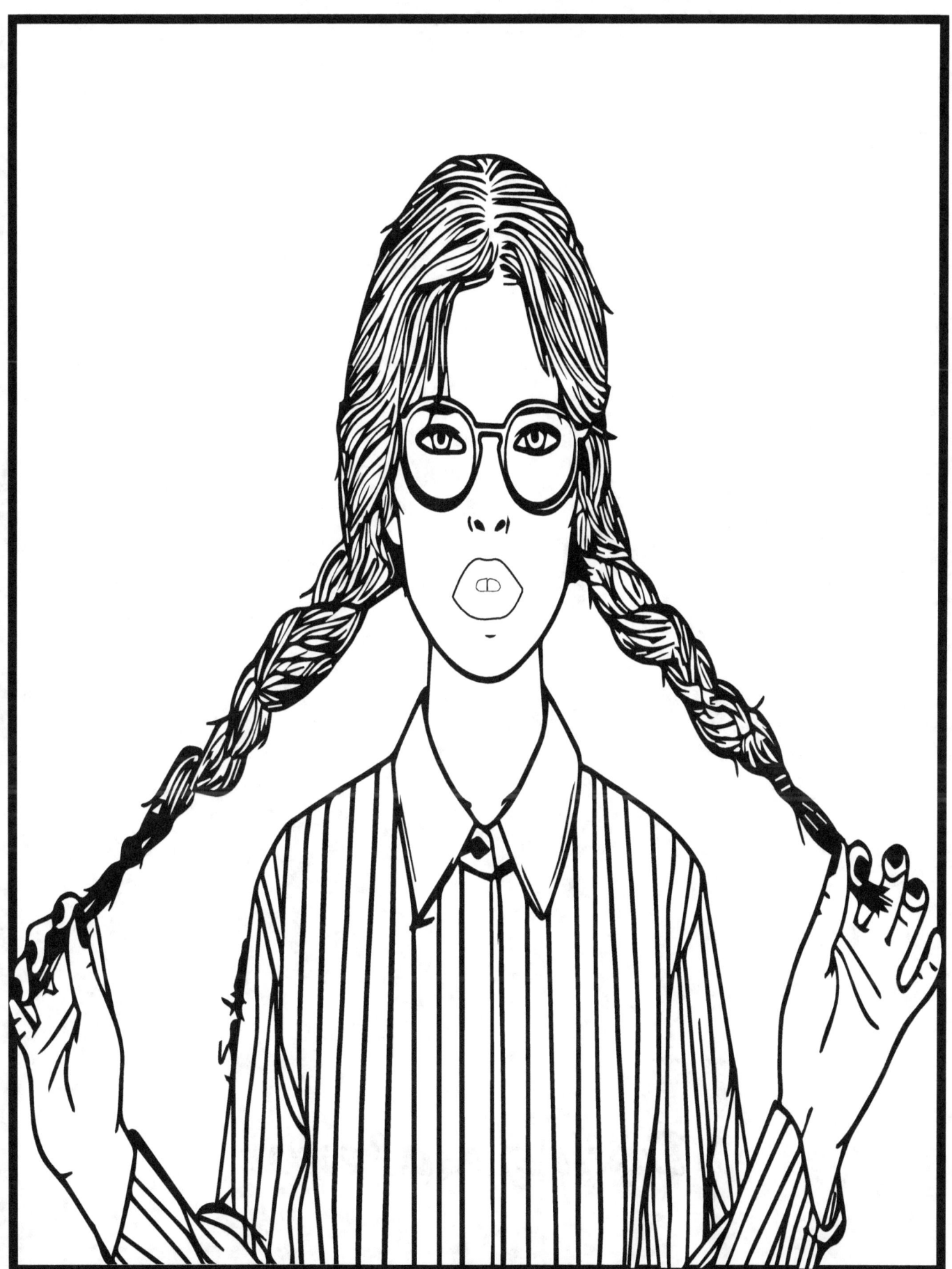

Daring makeup

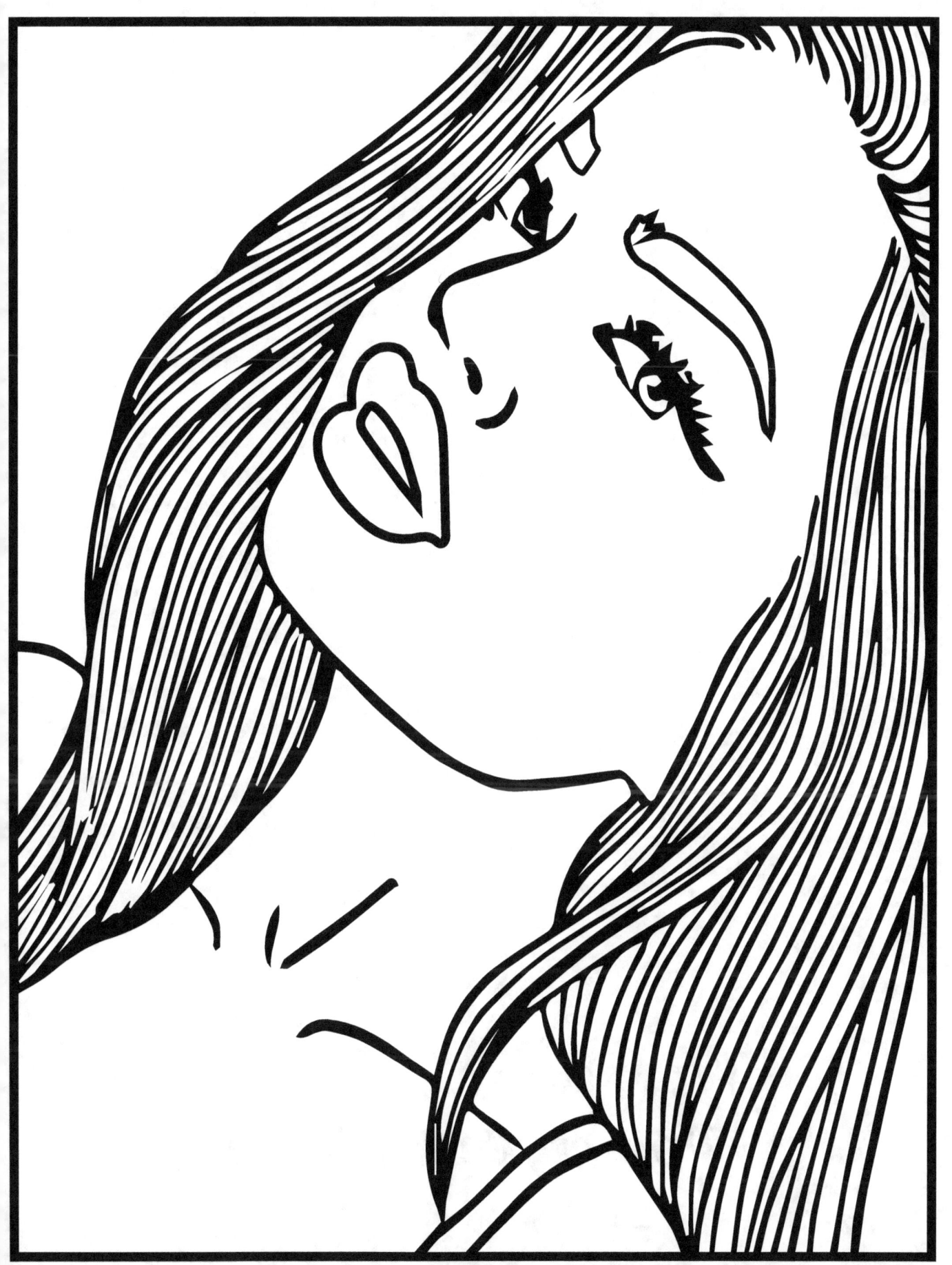

Pop style makeup

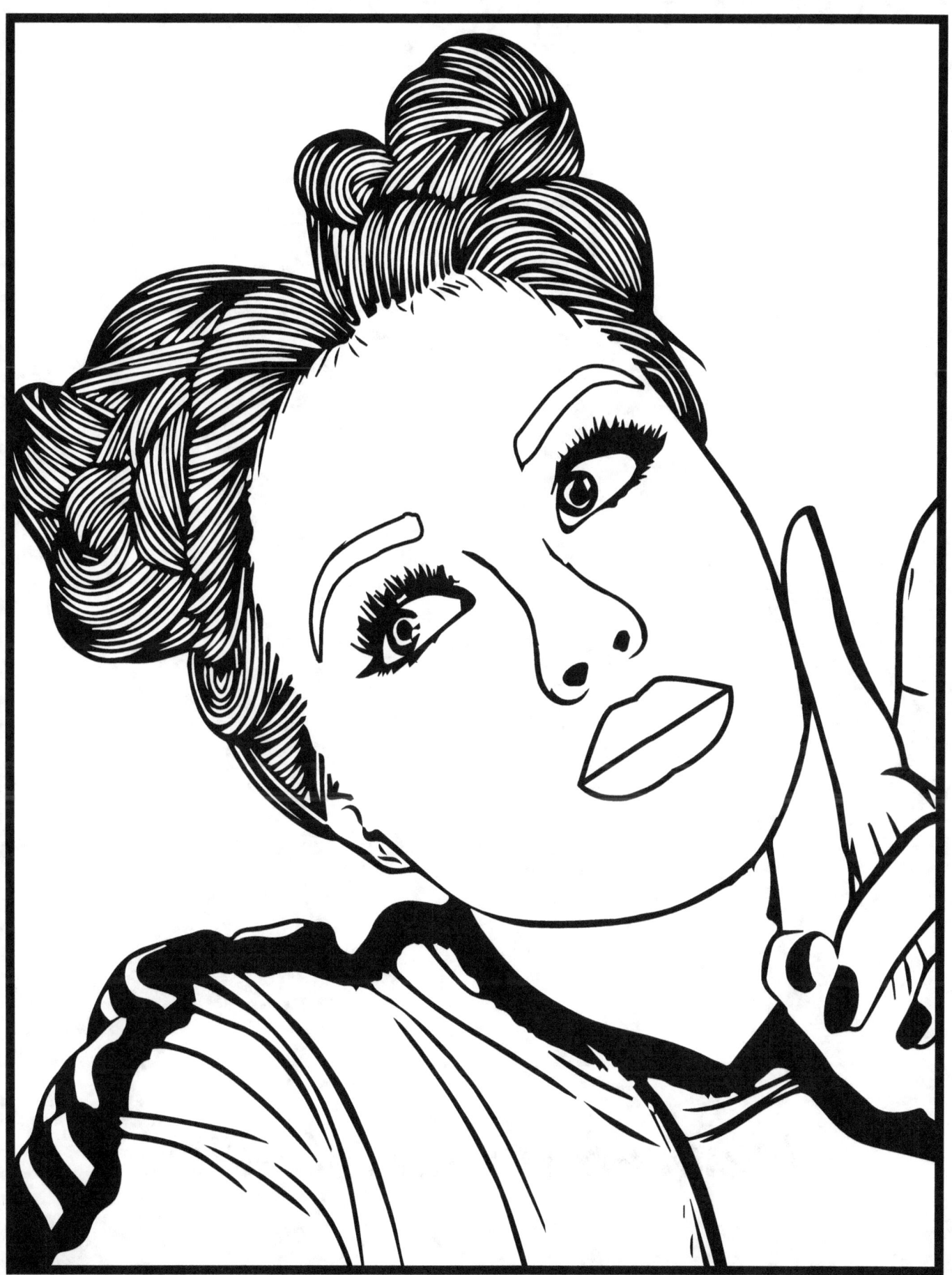

Makeup for an interview

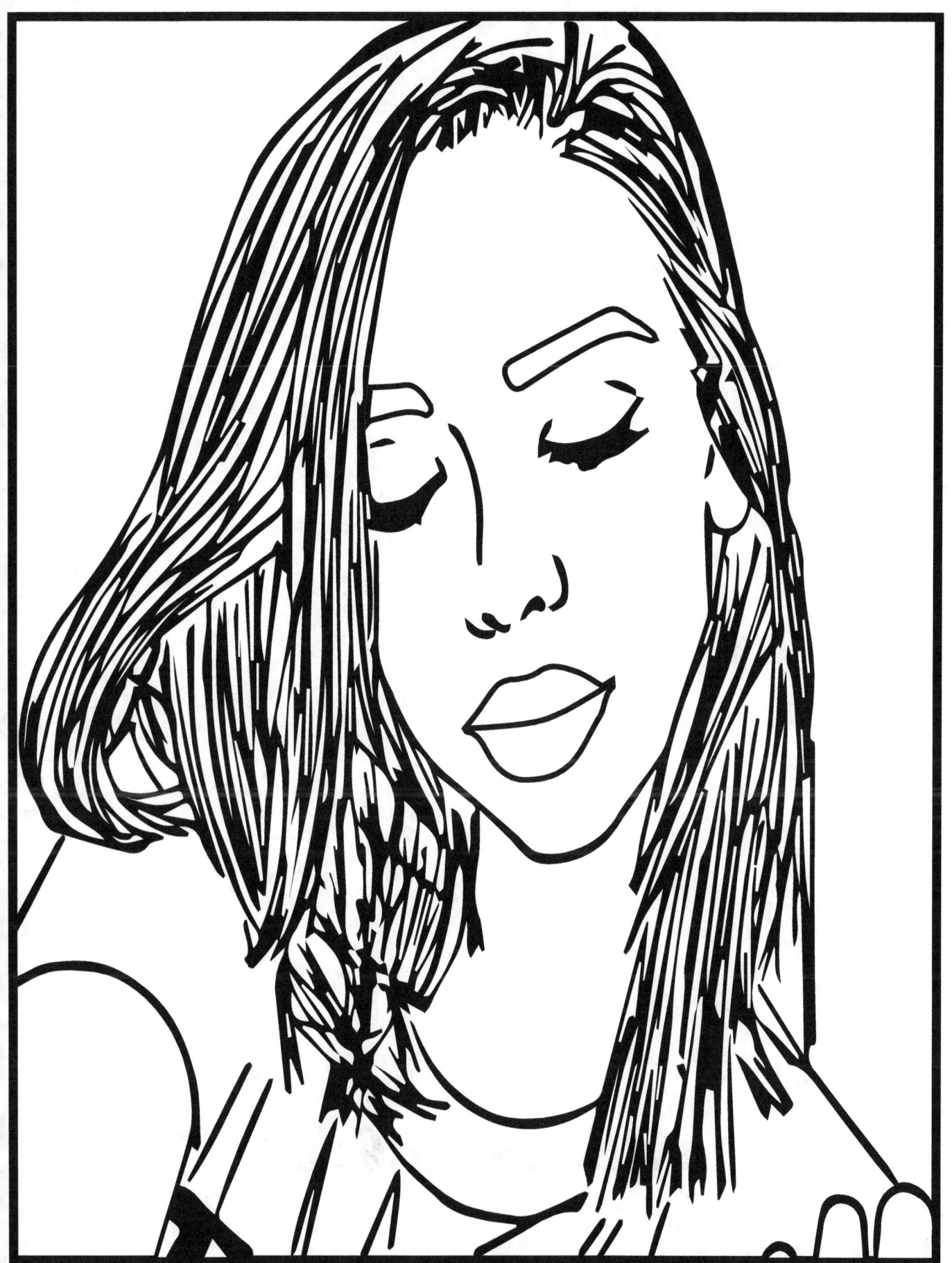

African makeup

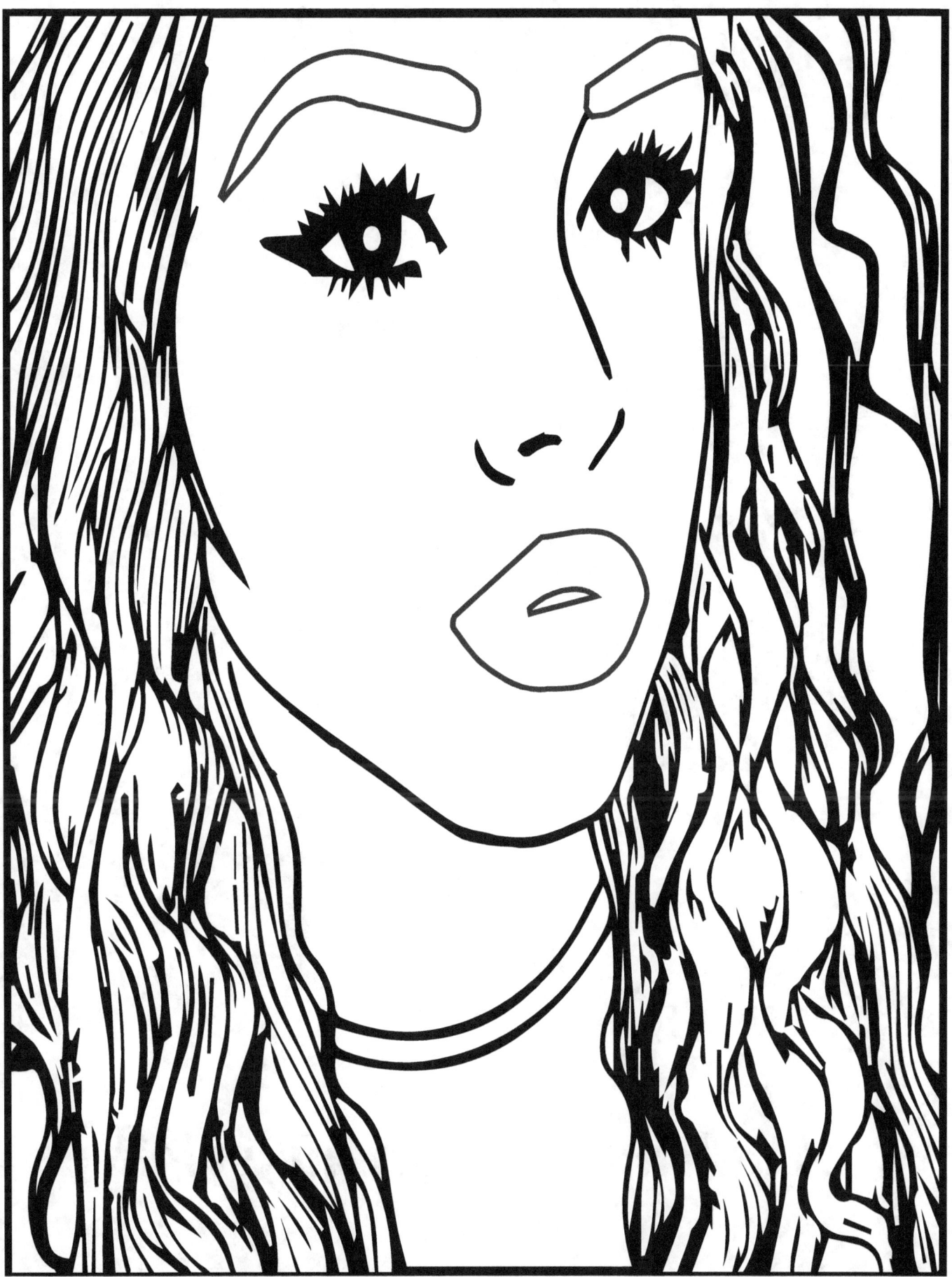

Makeup for a family visit

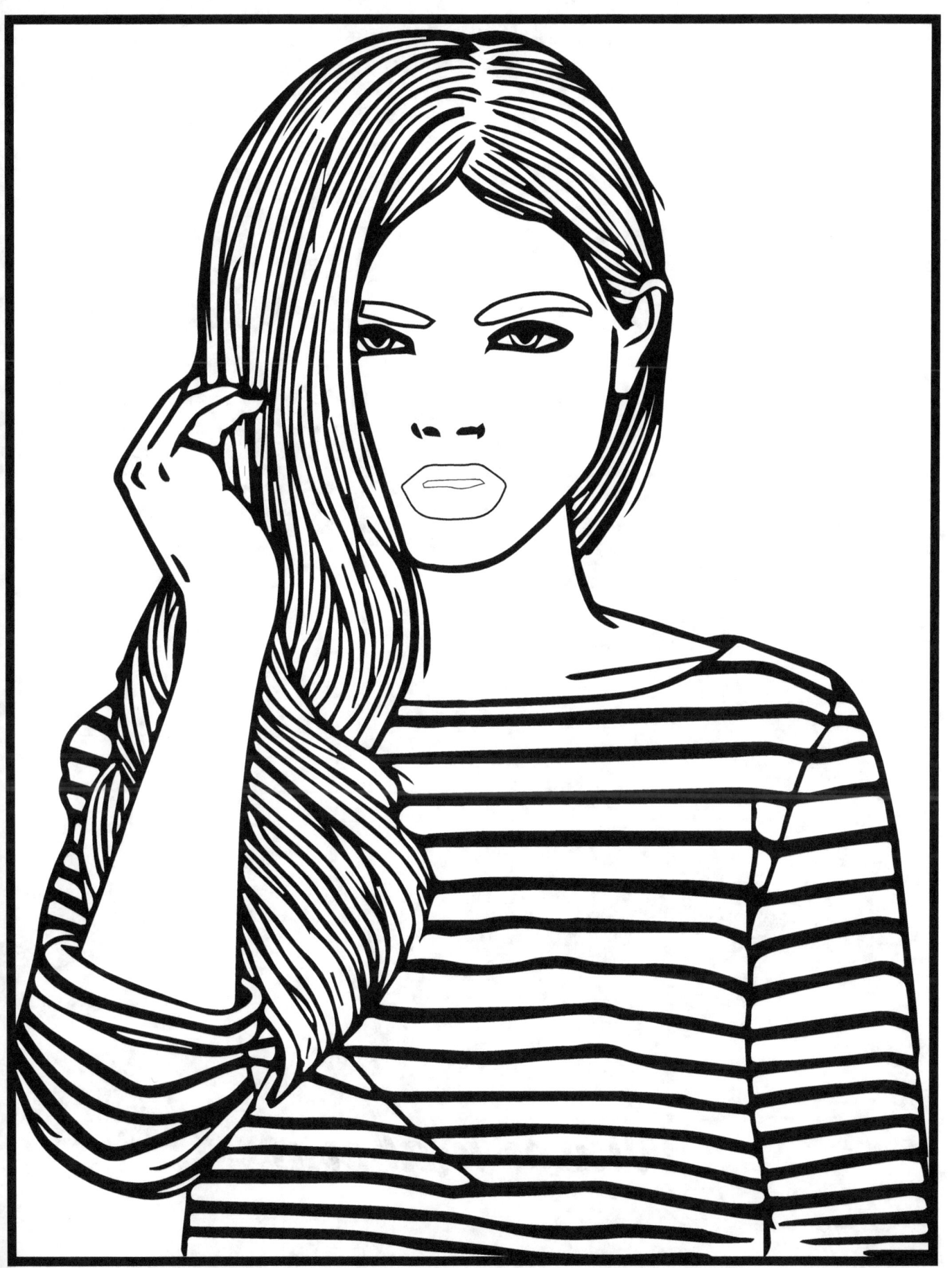

Winter makeup

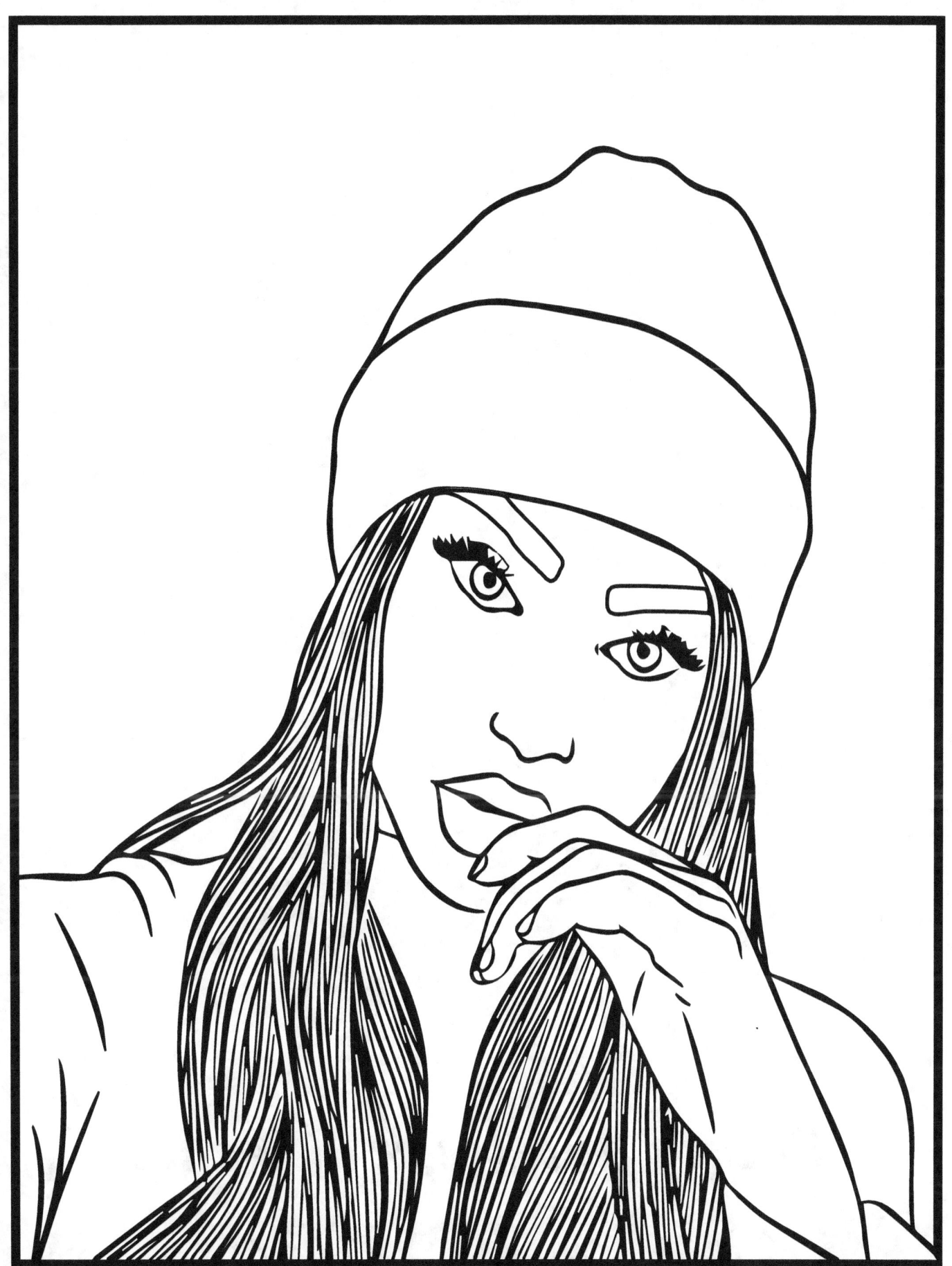

Sporty and fresh make-up

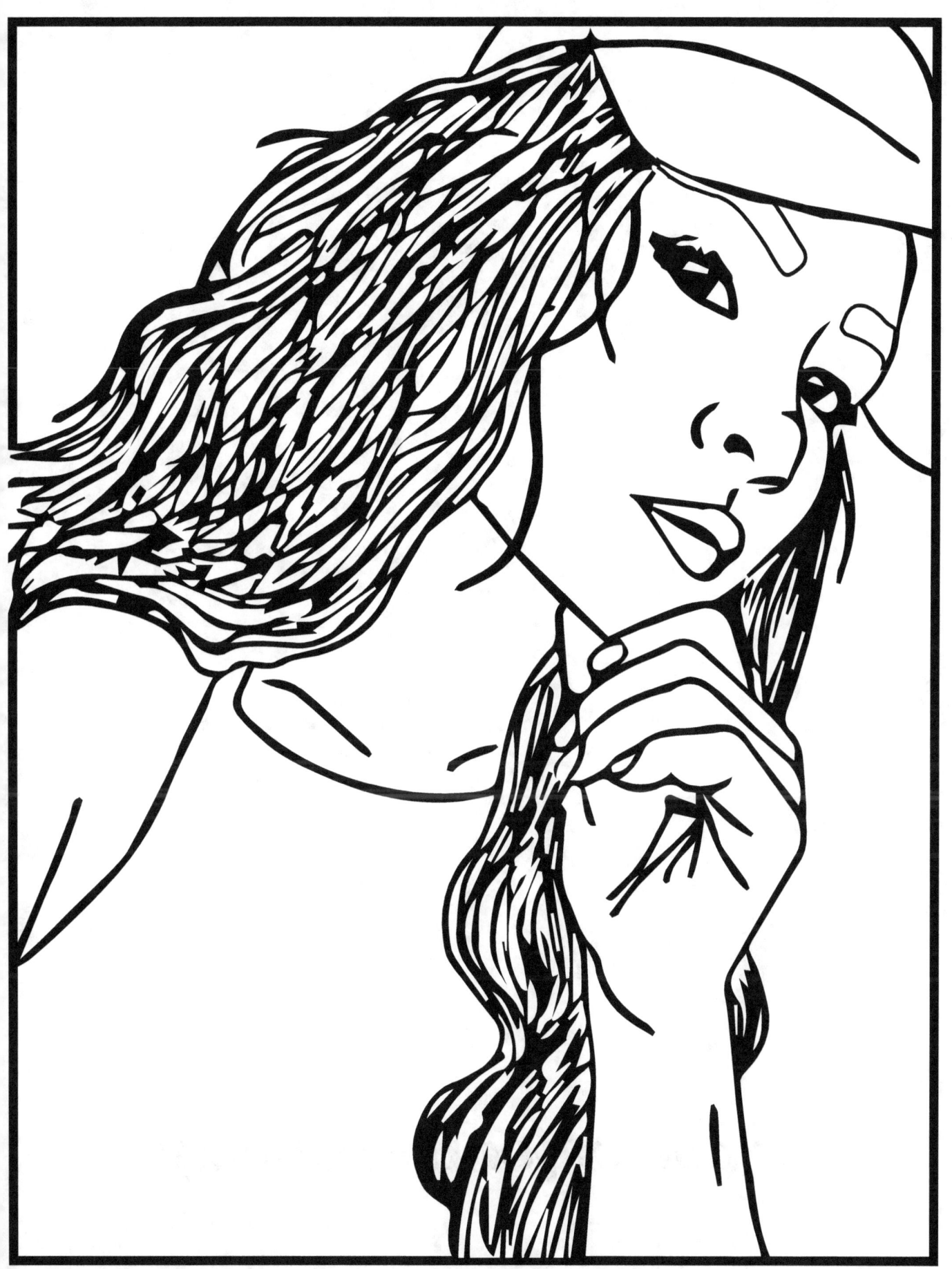

makeup for a ceremony

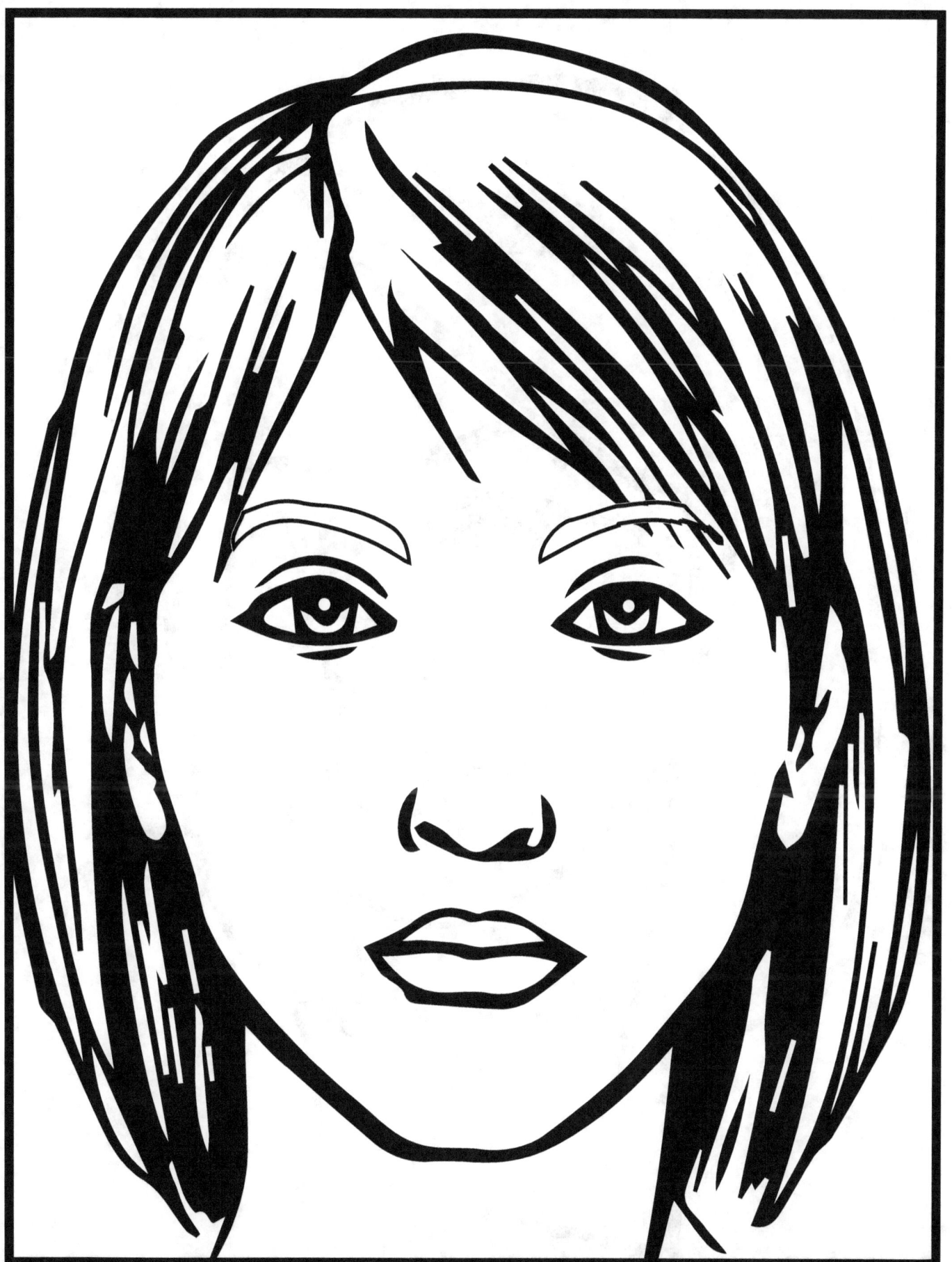

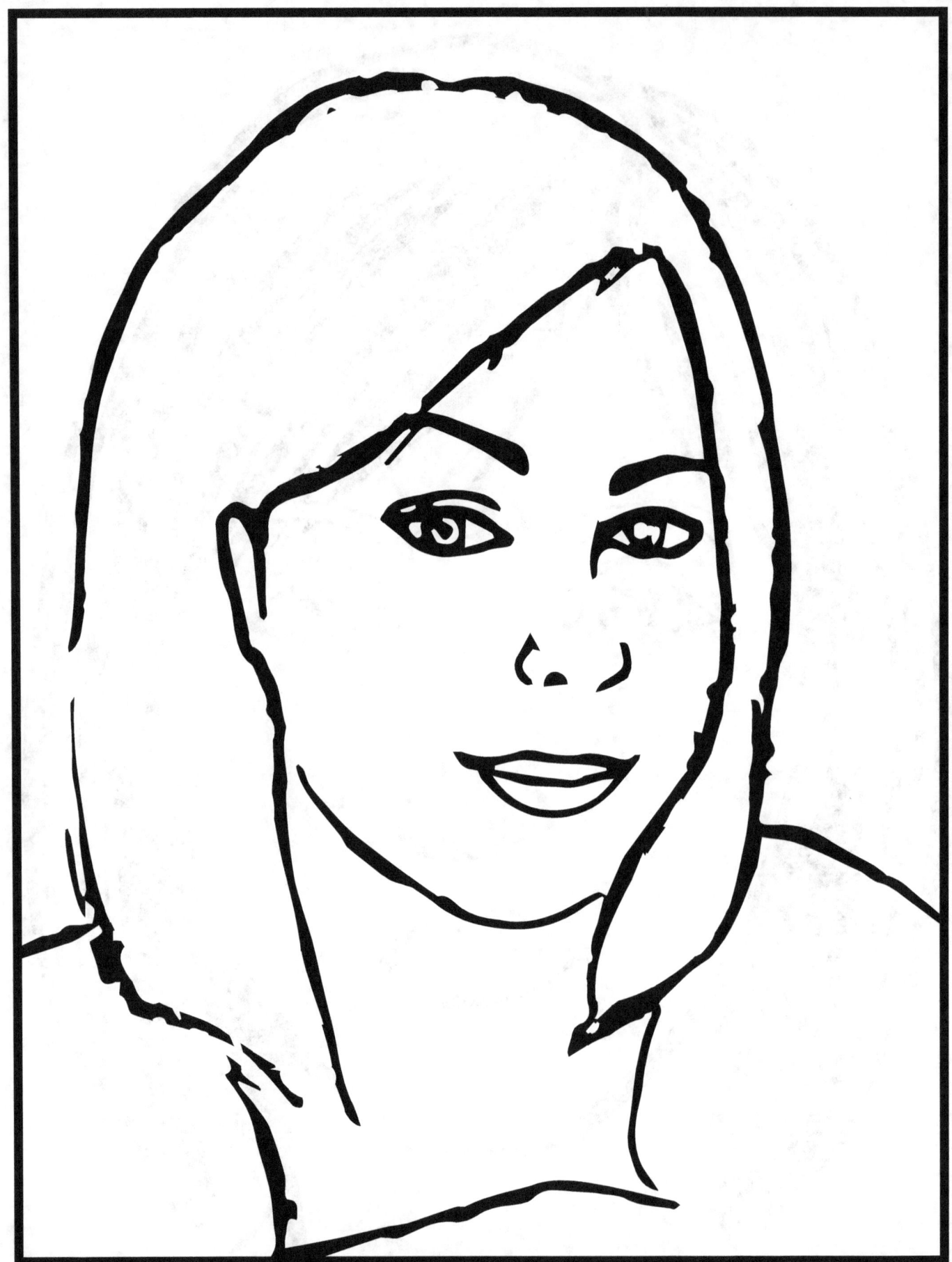

www.ingramcontent.com/pod-product-compliance
Lightning Source LLC
Chambersburg PA
CBHW081658220526
45466CB00009B/2811